June 10th 2001.

To   Todd
Happy birthda
with lots

Karen
xxx   x   xxx

CW01096005

Best Bible
STORIES

A SURPRISE FOR PETER

Jennifer Rees Larcombe

Illustrated by Steve Björkman

Marshall Pickering
An Imprint of HarperCollinsPublishers

Marshall Pickering is an Imprint of
HarperCollins*Religious*
Part of HarperCollins*Publishers*
77–85 Fulham Palace Road,
London W6 8JB
www.christian-publishing.co.uk

First published in 1992 in Great Britain
by Marshall Pickering as part of the
Children's Bible Story Book by Jennifer Rees Larcombe
This edition published in 2000 by Marshall Pickering

1 3 5 7 9 10 8 6 4 2

Text copyright © 1992, 2000 Jennifer Rees Larcombe
Illustrations copyright © 2000 Steve Björkman

Jennifer Rees Larcombe and Steve Björkman assert the moral right to be
identified as the author and illustrator of this work.

A catalogue record for this book is
available from the British Library.

ISBN 0 551 03246 4

Printed and bound in Hong Kong

A SURPRISE FOR PETER

'There'll be **no dinner** for the children **again** today,' sighed Peter as he and his brother **rowed ashore** one morning.

How was he going to tell his wife and grandmother that once again they had worked

all night **without catching a** single fish?

'Whatever's happening on the beach?' said Andrew. 'Who are all those people?'

'Jesus is back!' exclaimed their friends James and John.

'And it looks as if hundreds of people have come to hear him.'

Peter felt **really cross**.

He **longed** to rush up to his new friend and tell him all his worries, but **Jesus was hidden** in the middle of a great crowd of strangers.

'They won't be able to hear a word he says,' growled Peter, 'if they all **keep pushing** each other like that.' He had been fishing all night and he was **tired**.

But just as he was walking **miserably**
home he heard Jesus call his name.

'**Peter,** will you row me out
a little way in your boat?'

For **hours** they rocked
in the sunshine with Jesus sitting
where everyone on the beach could
see and hear him
perfectly.

Some of the stories he told were
so funny people ached with laughter,
while others made even the grown-ups cry.

'Thank you, Peter,' smiled Jesus at last.

'Now let's go fishing.'
'What!' exclaimed Peter.

'At midday?' and he burst out laughing.
This man might know a lot about carpentry,
but he certainly knew nothing about fishing.

'Please,' persisted Jesus.
'But you can't catch fish in this lake when the sun's shining,' grinned the fisherman.
'And anyway, there just aren't any fish about these days.'

Still Jesus sat there, **smiling,** until
in the end Peter and his brother had to
throw the nets over the side of the boat.

Almost at once an **extraordinary** thing happened. They caught such a huge shoal of fish the boat **nearly capsized!**

'**Come out here and help us!**' yelled Peter, waving frantically to James and John.

The nets were almost **breaking** as the four
fishermen dragged them out of the water,
and soon both the boats were

so full

of silvery fish they almost sank.

'I never saw such a catch in my life,' cried Peter, flinging himself down in front of Jesus. 'You shouldn't come near a man like me. I'm always breaking God's rules.'

'But God wants people to know how much he longs to forgive them,' said Jesus. 'Will you leave your fishing and help me to tell them all about God?'

Peter was so pleased he **hardly knew** what to say. 'I need to find twelve men who will be my **special** helpers,' said Jesus as he looked at Andrew, James and John. 'Will you come with me as well?' 'But we're only **fishermen**,' they gasped.

'I need **all kinds** of different people,' smiled Jesus. 'Now you go to market and sell those fish. You will make **enough money** to look after your families while you are away.'

Luke 5:1–11